Editor in Chief
Ina Massler Levin, M.A.

Editor
Eric Migliaccio

Contributing Editor
Sarah Smith

Creative Director
Karen J. Goldfluss, M.S. Ed.

Cover Design
Tony Carrillo / Marilyn Goldberg

Teacher Created Resources
12621 Western Avenue
Garden Grove, CA 92841
www.teachercreated.com

ISBN: 978-1-4206-5916-0

Reprinted, 2022 (PO604206)
Made in U.S.A.

Teacher Created Resources

This book belongs to

____

Ready·Set·Learn

Get Ready to Learn!

Get ready, get set, and go! Boost your child's learning with this exciting series of books. Geared to help children practice and master many needed skills, the *Ready·Set·Learn* books are bursting with 64 pages of learning fun. Use these books for . . .

- enrichment
- skills reinforcement
- extra practice

With their smaller size, the *Ready·Set·Learn* books fit easily in children's hands, backpacks, and book bags. All your child needs to get started are pencils, crayons, and colored pencils.

A full sheet of colorful stickers is included. Use these stickers for . . .

- decorating pages
- rewarding outstanding effort
- keeping track of completed pages

Celebrate your child's progress by using these stickers on the reward chart located on the inside cover. The blue-ribbon sticker fits perfectly on the certificate on page 64.

With *Ready·Set·Learn* and a little encouragement, your child will be on the fast track to learning fun!

Twins

Directions: Count by twos to figure out how many people are on the page.

____

____

____

____

____

____

____

____

____

________ people

Snowflakes

Directions: Count by twos to finish the number pattern. Color in the snowflakes that have the numbers in the pattern.

2, 4, 6...

Granola Bars

Directions: There are two granola bars in each package. Count by twos to figure out how many granola bars are in the box.

____

____

____

____

____

____

_______ granola bars

Joining the Dots by 2s

Directions: Here is a hidden picture. Count by 2s to connect the dots. What do you see?

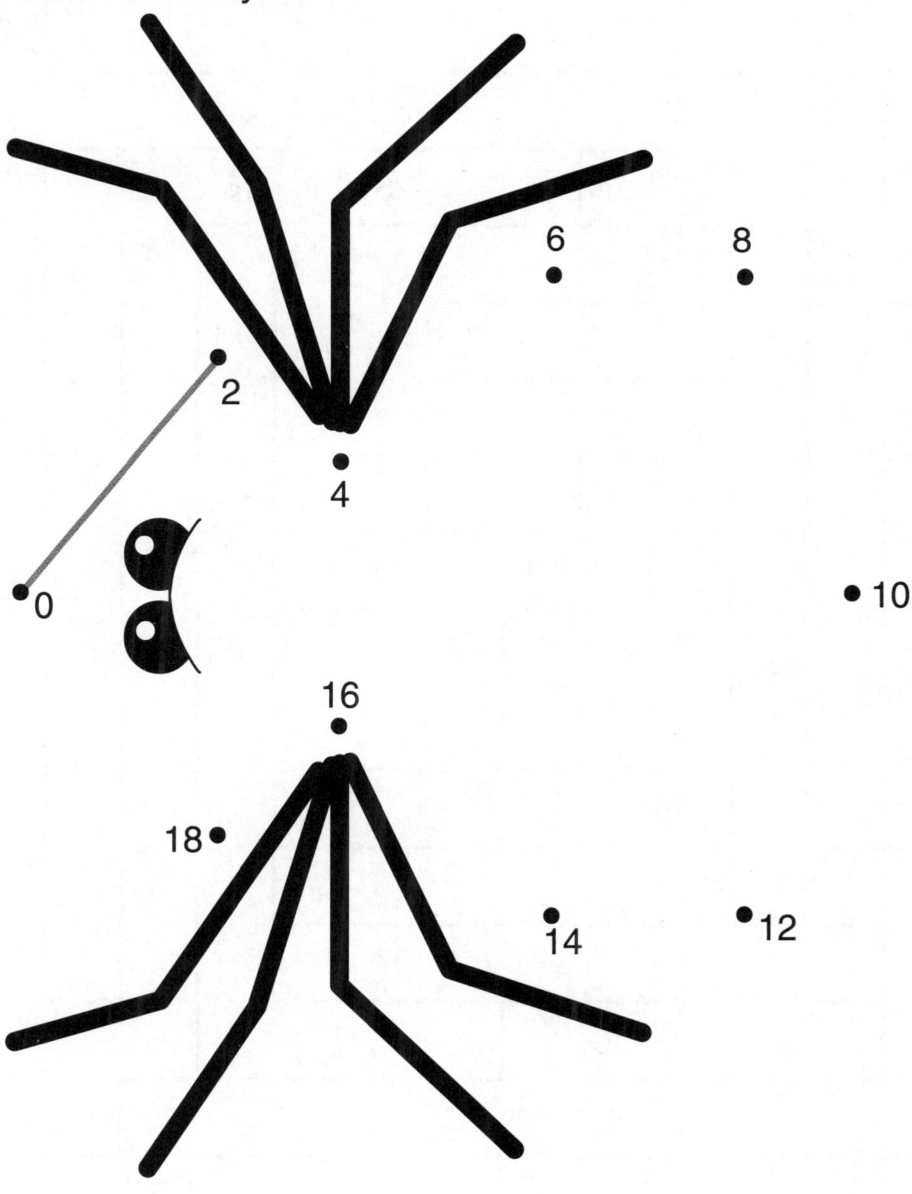

Counting Up by 2s

Directions: Follow the path of numbers that count up by 2s.

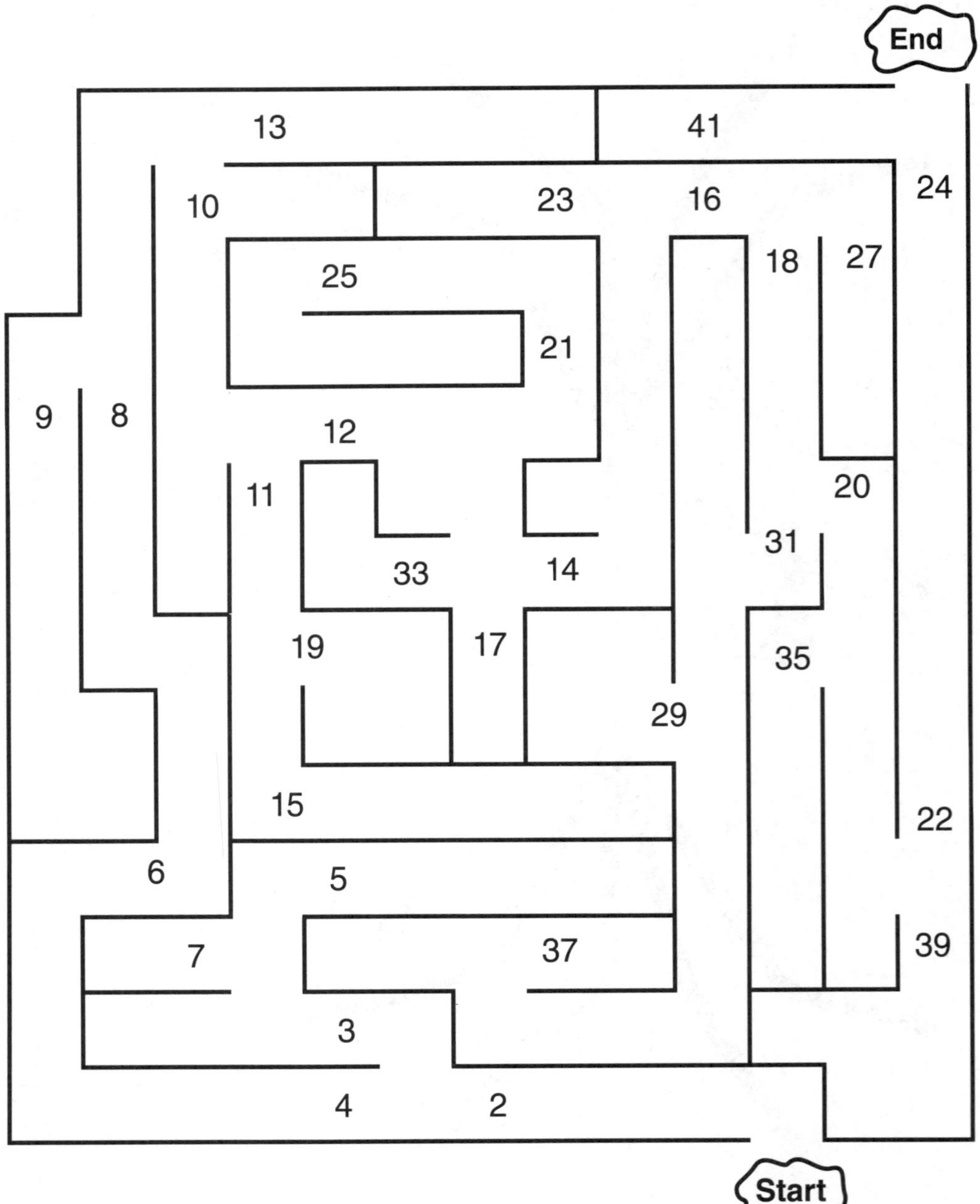

Wizard Hats

Directions: Start by coloring in the hat with the number 6. Then, continue counting by twos to figure out which other hats to color.

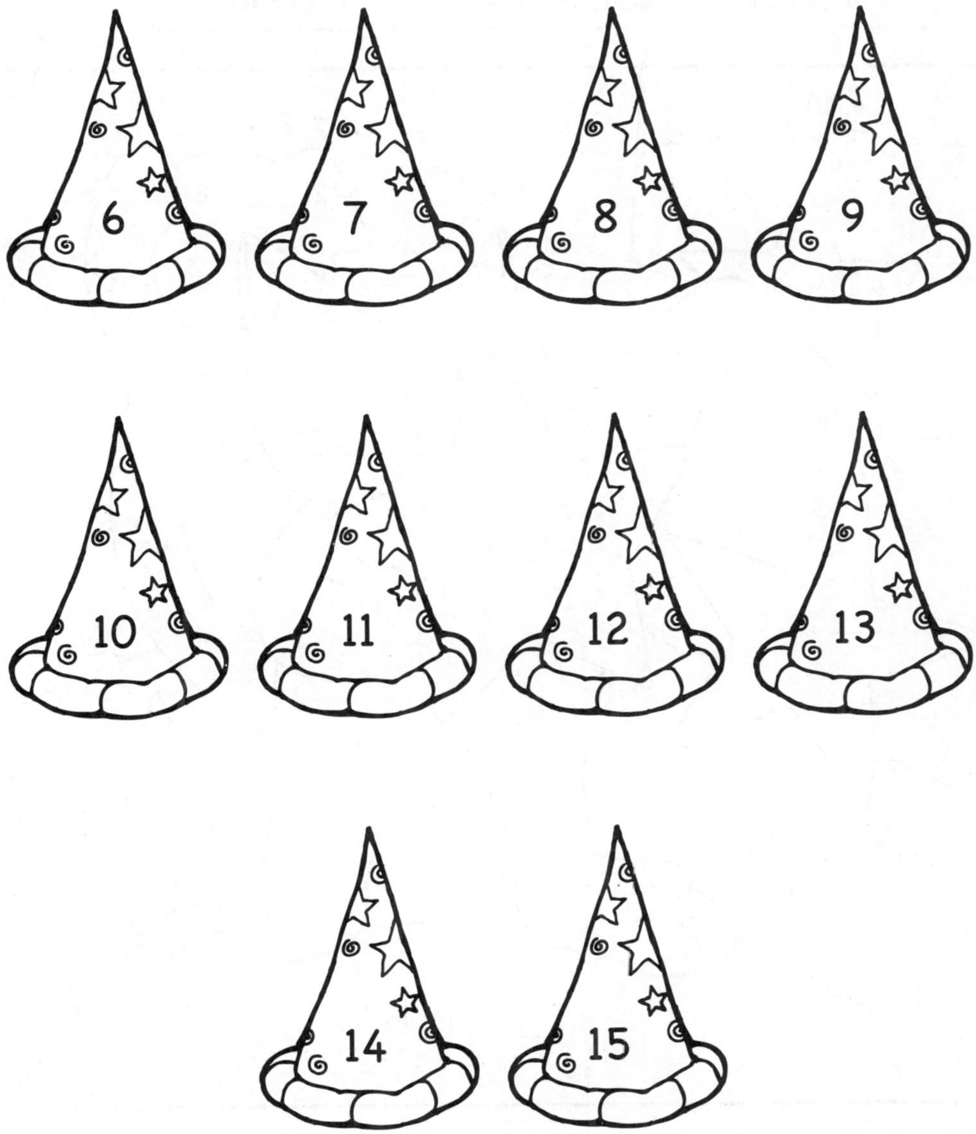

By the 2s

Directions: Complete each number pattern. Color the puzzle.

2 = yellow	**4 = purple**	**6 = blue**	**8 = green**	**10 = red**

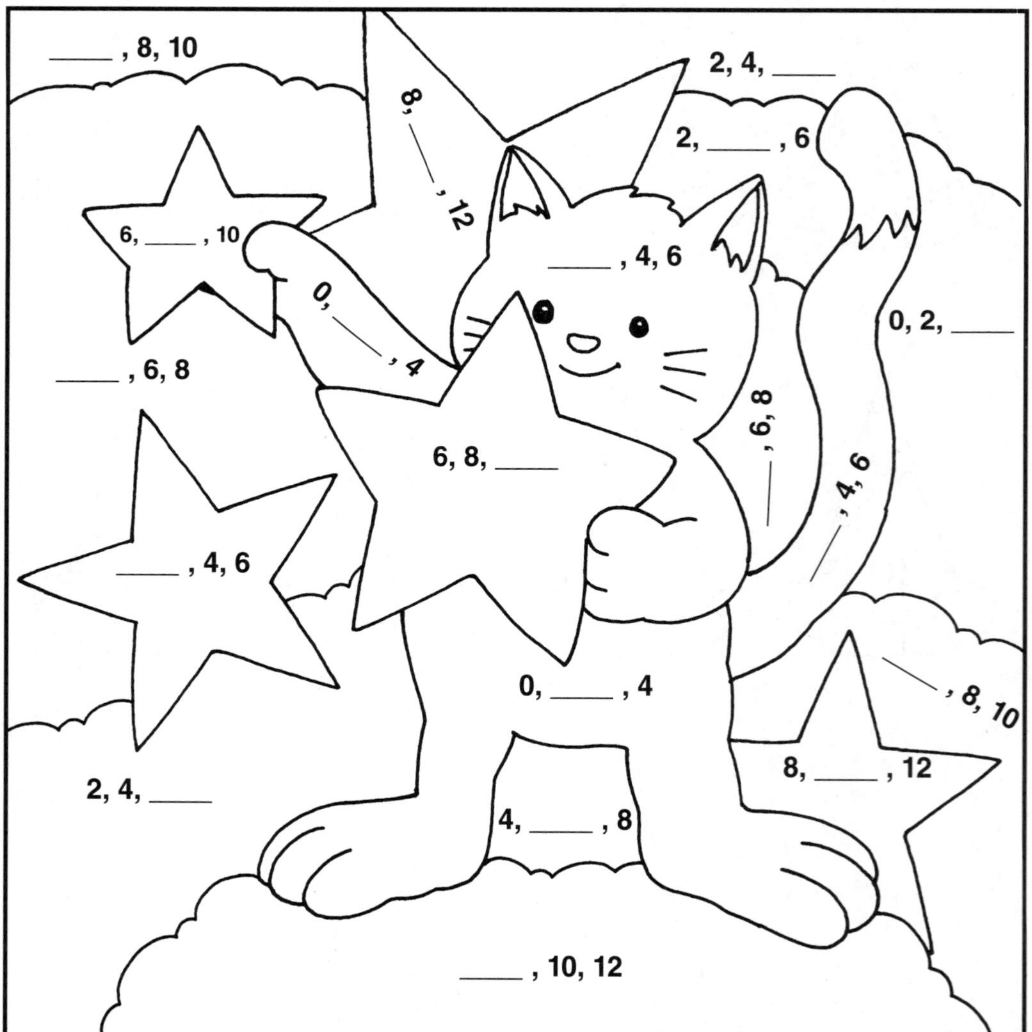

Pond Life

Directions: Color in the animal that finishes the number pattern in each row.

2, 4, 6...

5, 7, 9...

8, 10, 12...

15, 17, 19...

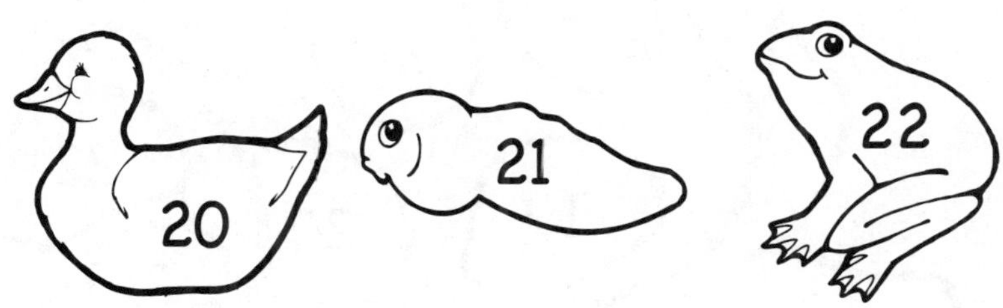

22, 24, 26...

Giraffe

Directions: Finish the number pattern by coloring in the correct answers in the giraffe's spots.

1, 3, 5...

Fabulous Twos

Directions: Count by twos to finish the pattern. Write the number in the blank.

2		6		
	14			20
22			28	
32		36		
	44			50

Bubbles

Directions: Color in the bubbles that finish the number pattern.

52, 54, 56...

Seeing Double

Directions: Start at the number 2 and count by twos to discover the hidden pictures.

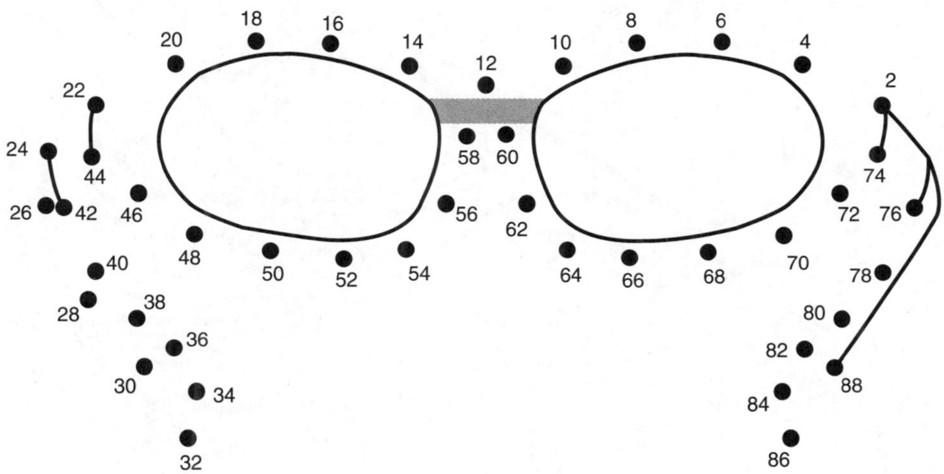

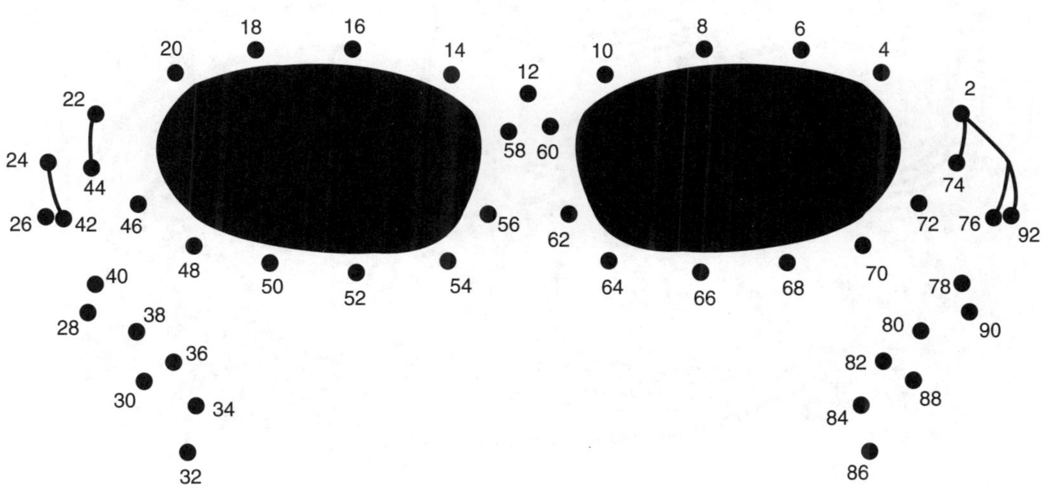

Ducks on a Pond

Directions: Color in the ducks that finish the number pattern.

81, 83, 85...

Pumpkin Pie

Directions: Finish the number pattern by coloring in the pie slices that have the numbers in the pattern.

3, 6, 9...

Magic Beans

Directions: Count by threes to figure out how many magic beans are on the page!

How many magic beans are there? ________

Triceratops

Directions: Count by threes to figure out how many horns are on the page.

______ ______ ______

______ ______ ______

______ ______

Paint Cans

Directions: Finish the number pattern by coloring in the paint cans that have the correct numbers on them.

9, 12, 15...

Honey Bees

Directions: Count by threes to figure out how many bees are busy making honey.

________ ________ ________ ________

________ ________ ________ ________

________ ________ ________

How many bees are busy making honey? ________

Out of This World

Directions: Aliens with three eyes have invaded your worksheet! Count the eyes on each alien by threes to find the number of eyes that are watching you.

1.  = ________ eyes

2.  = ________ eyes

3.  = ________ eyes

4.  = ________ eyes

5.  = ________ eyes

Bean Jar

Directions: Finish the number pattern by coloring in the correct answers in the bean jar.

3, 6, 9...

Flying South

Directions: These birds fly together in fours. Count by fours to figure out how many birds are flying south for the winter.

____

____

____

____

____

____

____

_______ birds

Crayons

Directions: Finish the number pattern by coloring in the crayons with the correct answers.

4, 8, 12...

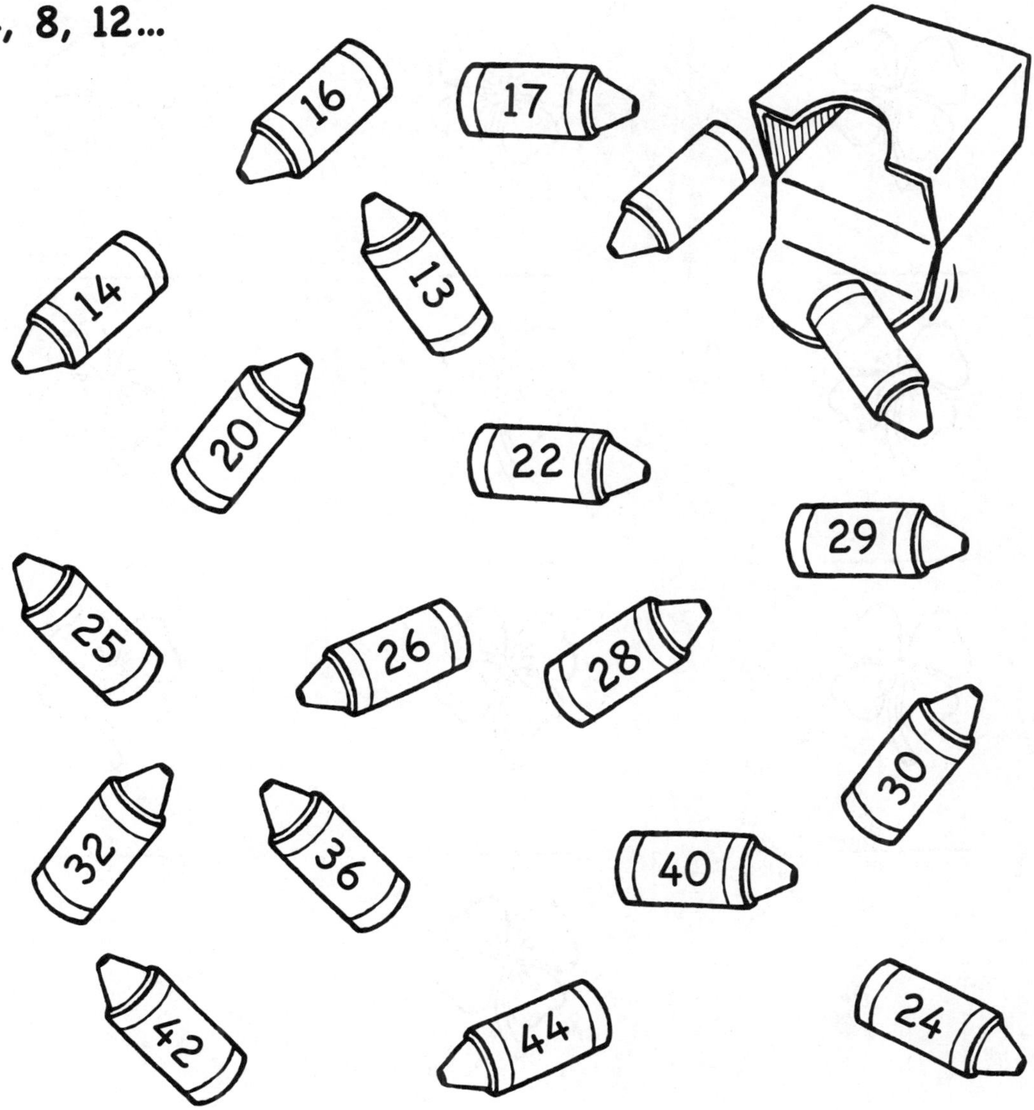

Lucky Clovers

Directions: Count by fours to figure out how many clover leaves are on the page.

____

____

____

____

____

____

____

____

____

____

________ clover leaves

Fall Leaves

Directions: Finish the number pattern by coloring in the leaves with the correct answers.

12, 16, 20...

Tomato Plants

Directions: Count by fours to figure out how many tomatoes are growing in the garden.

__________ __________

____

__________ __________

__________ tomatoes

Keys

Directions: Count by fives to see how many keys are hanging on the key rings.

________ ________ ________ ________

________ ________ ________ ________

________ ________

________ keys

Pick Which One

Directions: Look at each group of items. Circle the group that can be counted by fives.

1. a.

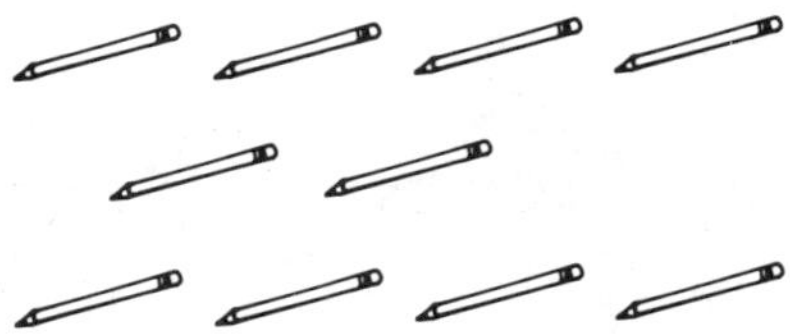

b.

2. a.

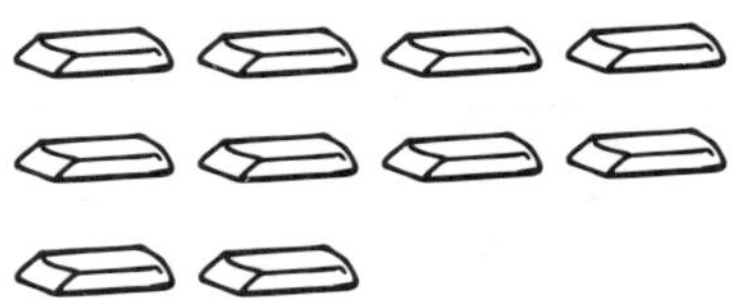

b.

3. a.

b.

4. a.

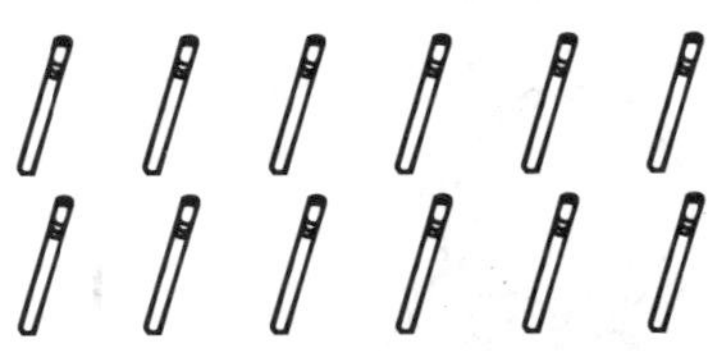

b.

5. a.

b.

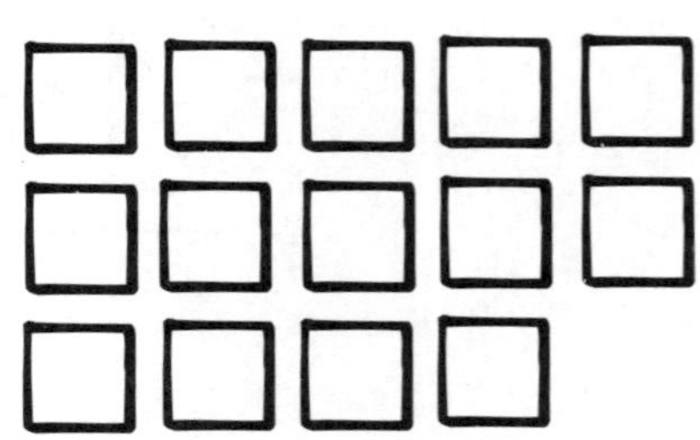

Counting Up by 5s

Directions: Follow the path of numbers that count up by 5s.

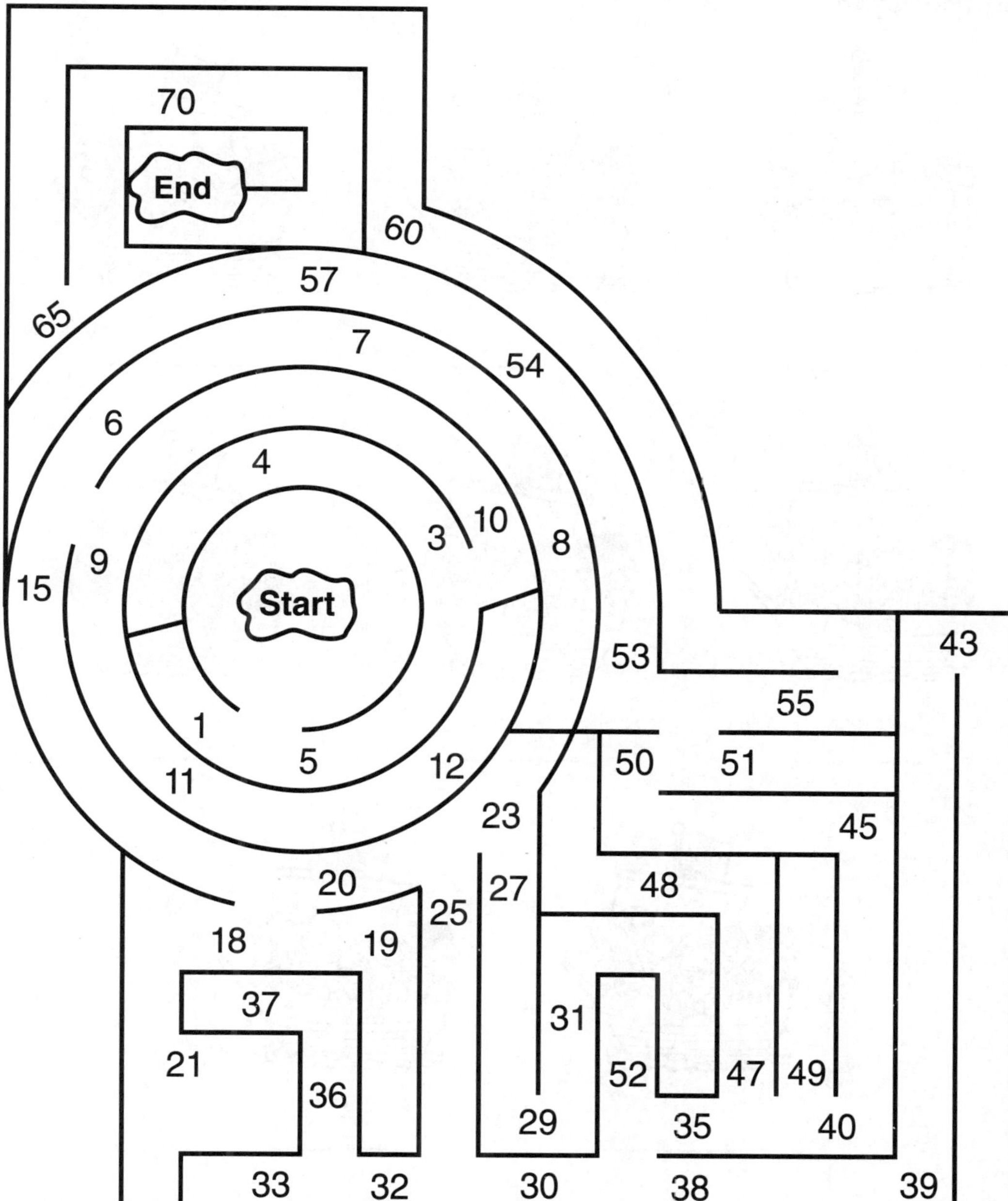

Ready·Set·Learn

Pirates

Directions: Count by fives to figure out how many pirates are on the seas.

____

____

____

____

____

____

____

____

________ pirates

It's Heavy!

Directions: Complete each number pattern. Color the puzzle.

5 = red   10 = blue   15 = green   20 = purple   25 = brown

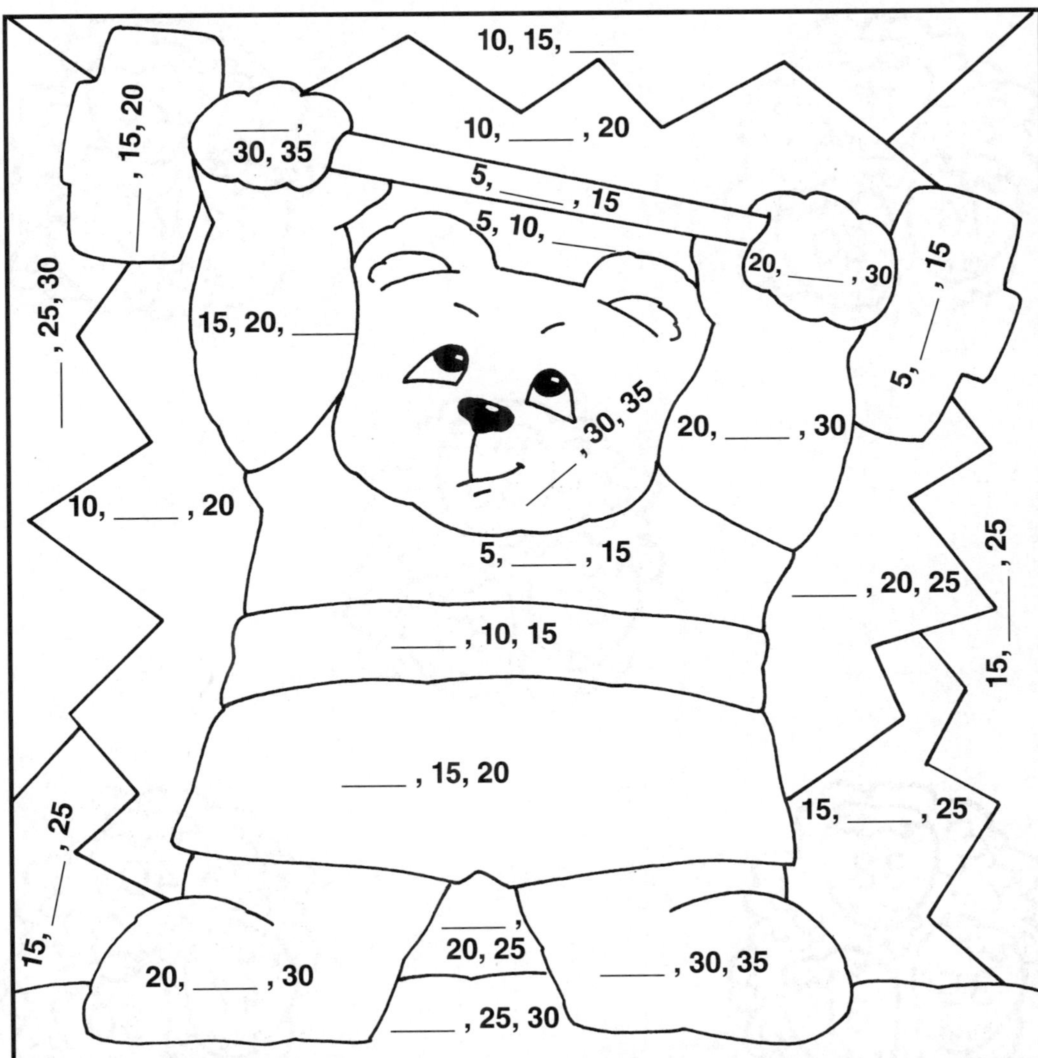

Strawberry Patch

Directions: Finish the number pattern by coloring in the strawberries with the correct answers.

5, 10, 15...

Counting by 5s

Directions: Some things might come in 5s, like fingers on a hand or toes on a foot. There are 5 fingers on 1 hand, and there are 10 fingers on 2 hands. Count by 5 and write the numbers that tell you how many things there are altogether.

How many fingers?

5 10 15 20 25

How many crayons?

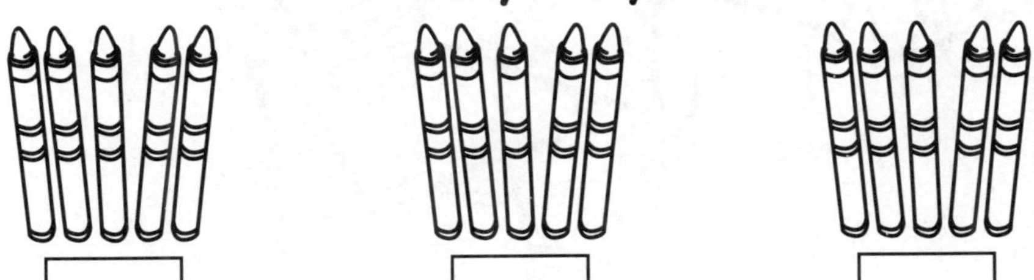

How many beads?

Page Numbers

Directions: Finish the pattern by numbering the pages that have fallen out of the book.

Fabulous Fives

Directions: Count by fives to finish the pattern. Write the correct numbers in the blank boxes.

5		15		
	35			50
		65	70	
80			95	

Clock

Directions: Finish the number pattern on the clock.

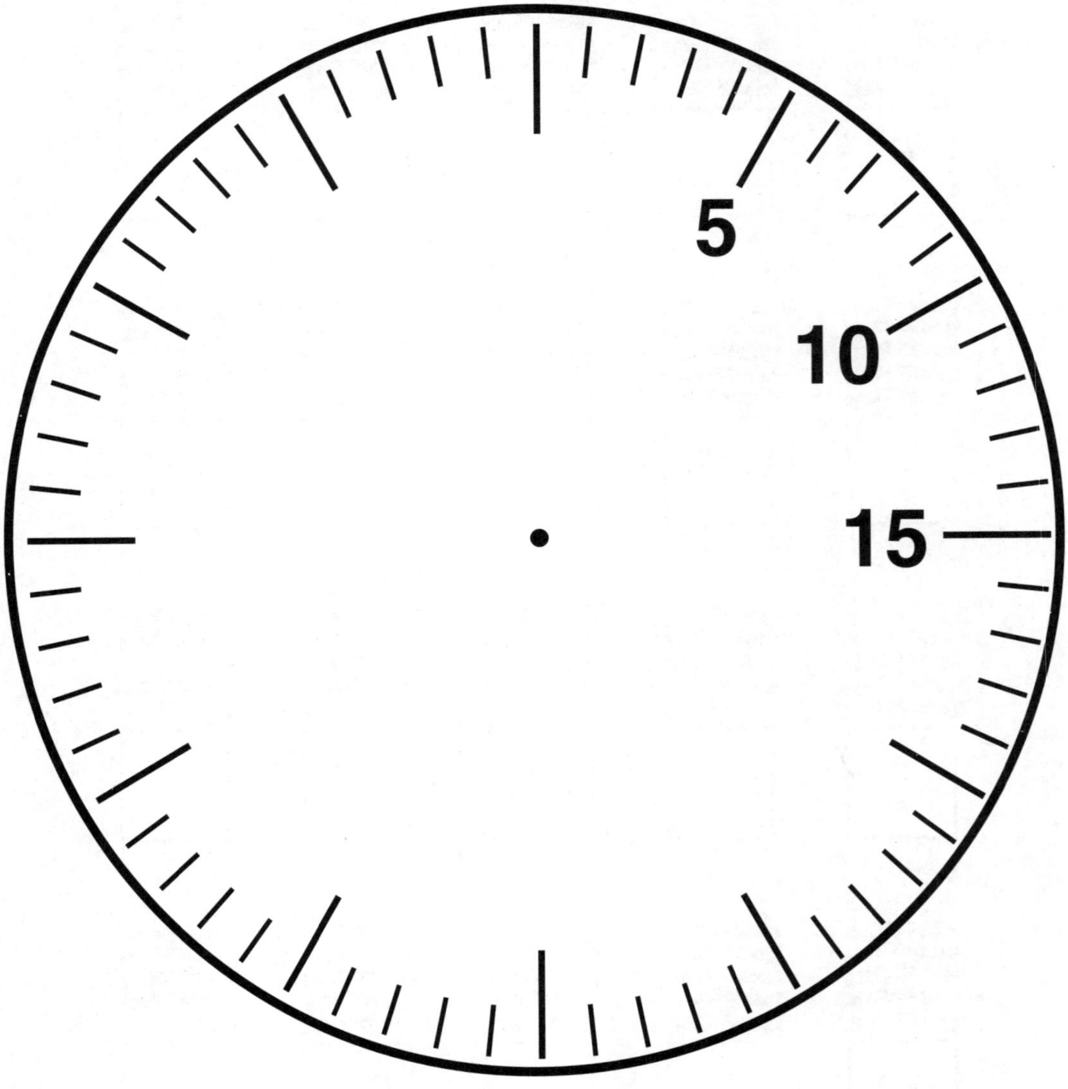

Counting by 5s

Directions: Help Max get home by counting by 5s.

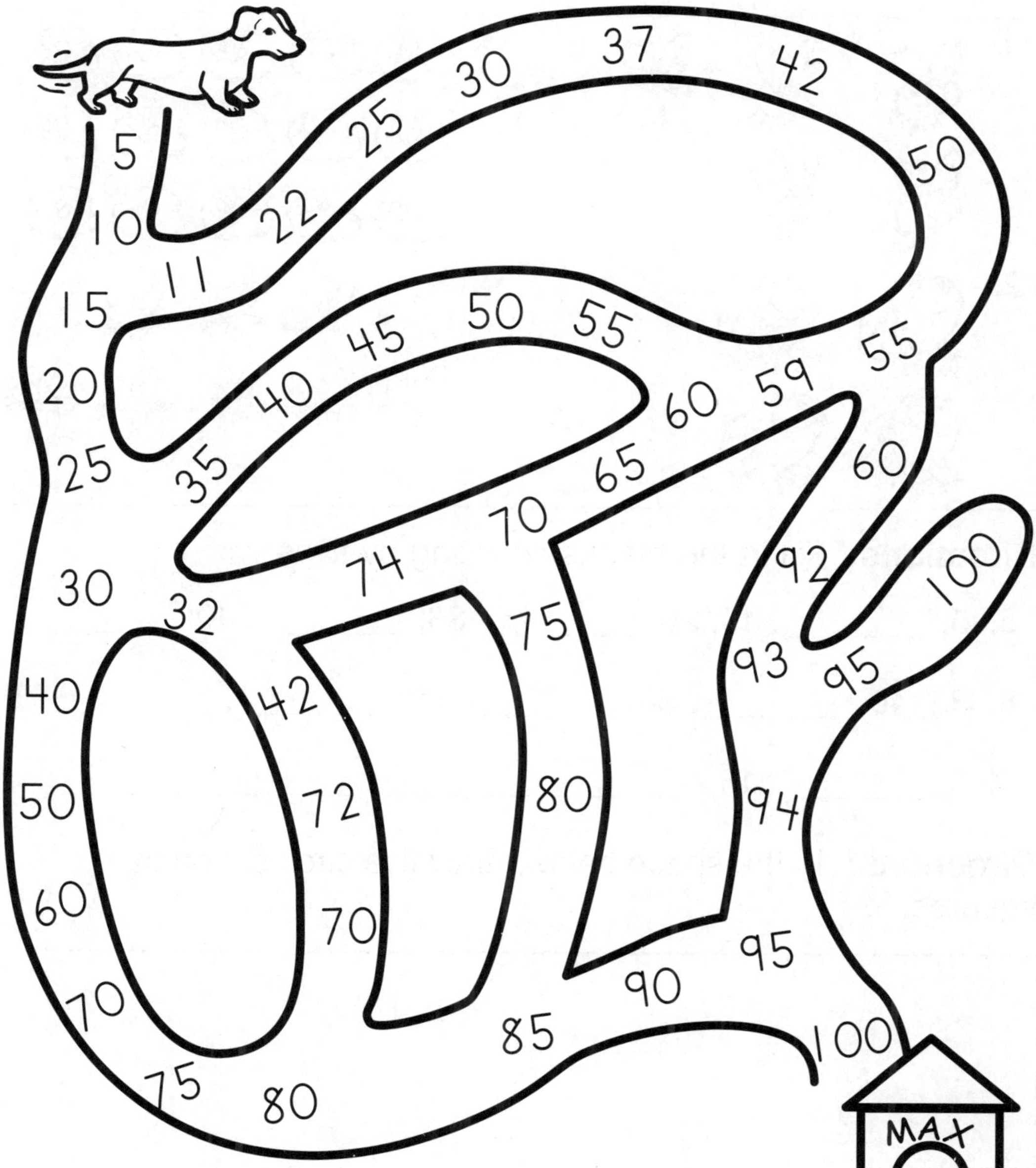

Five, Ten, Fifteen, Twenty

Directions: Circle the things that you can count by fives.

1. 

2. 

3. 

4. 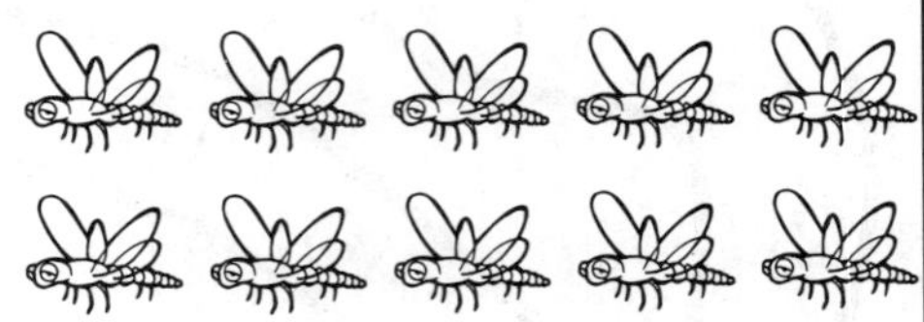

Directions: Fill in the blanks counting by fives.

5. 5, ________ , 15, 20, ________ , 30, ________ , 40, ________

6. 35, 40, ________ , 50, ________ , 60, ________ , ________ , 75

7. 5, ________ , 15, ________ , ________ , ________ , ________

Directions: In the space below, draw five circles, and five squares.

Veggies

Directions: There are five vegetables in each bag. Count by fives to see how many vegetables there are.

____

____

____

____

____

____

____

____

_______ vegetables

Fingers

Directions: Each pair of hands has 10 fingers. Count by tens to find out how many fingers are on the page.

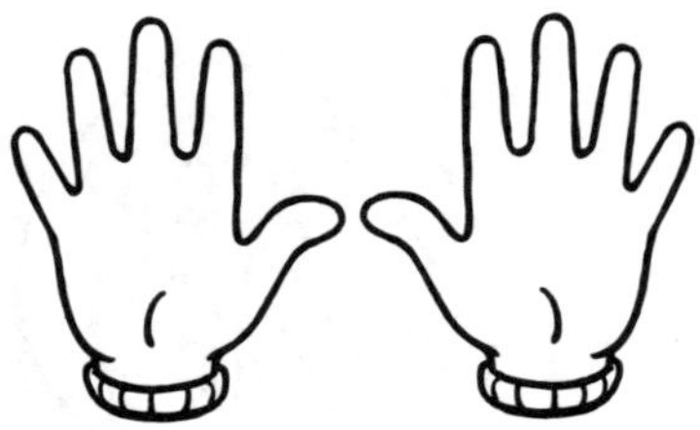

______

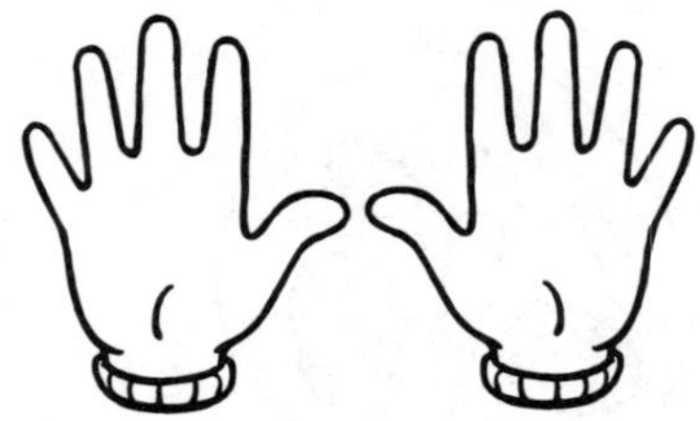

______

______

______

______

________ fingers

Groceries

Directions: There are ten cans in each grocery bag. Count by tens to figure out how many cans there are on the page.

____

____

____

____

____

____

____

____

____

____

________ cans

Tasty Tens

Directions: There are 10 cookies in each pile. Count the cookies and write the missing numbers in the boxes.

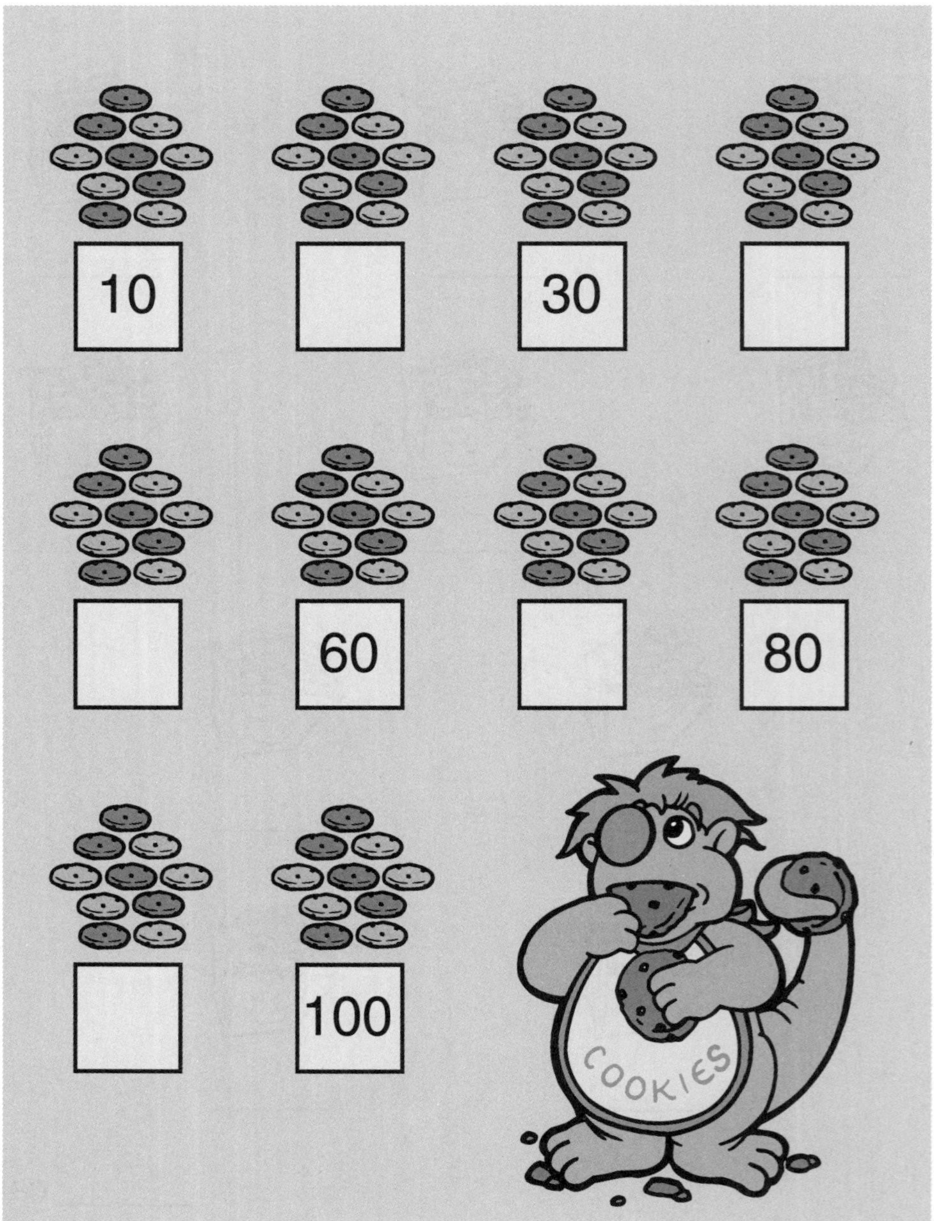

The Ants Go Marching

Directions: There are 10 ones in the number 10.

1 + 1 + 1 + 1 + 1 + 1 + 1 + 1 + 1 + 1 = 10

Circle the things at the picnic that are in groups of 10.

Lollipops

Directions: Draw 10 polka dots on each lollipop. Then count by tens to figure out how many dots you drew.

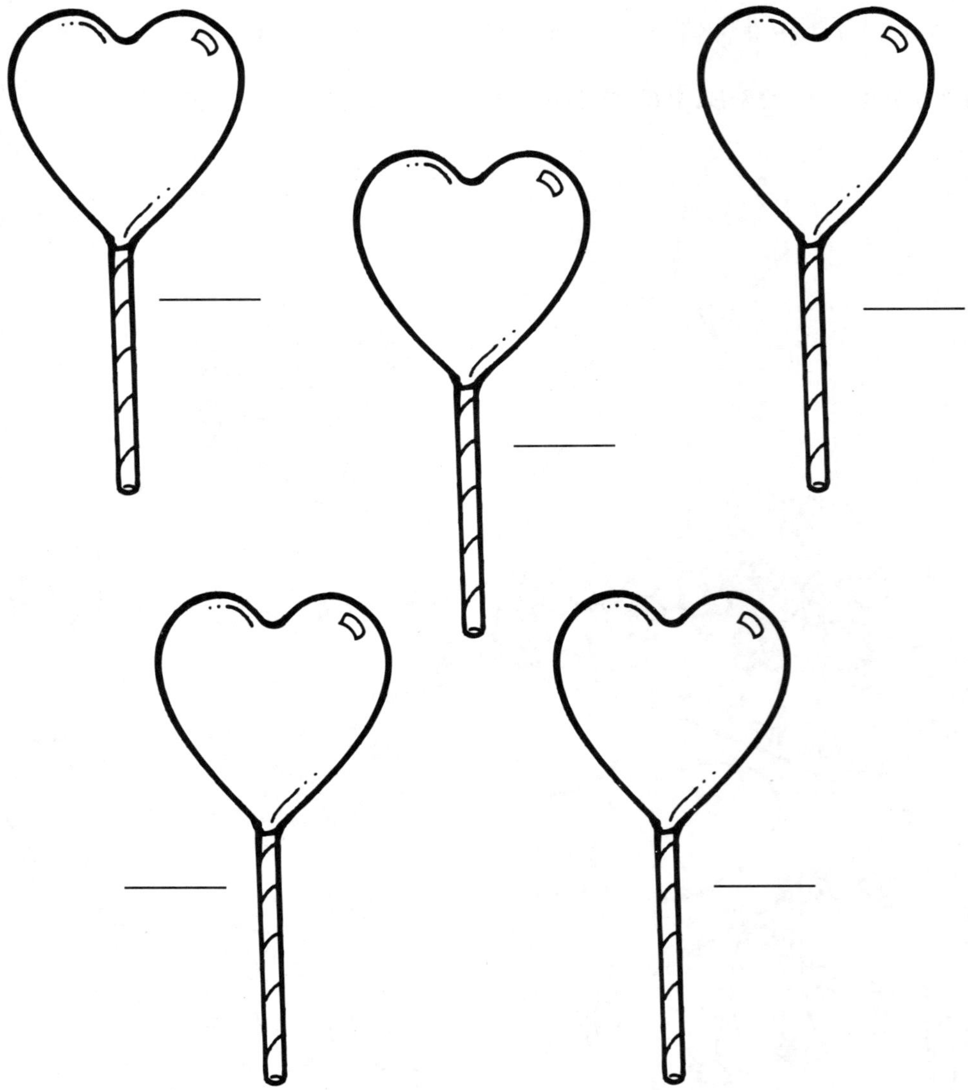

_______ polka dots

Counting by 10s

Directions: Count by 10s to complete the dot-to-dot.

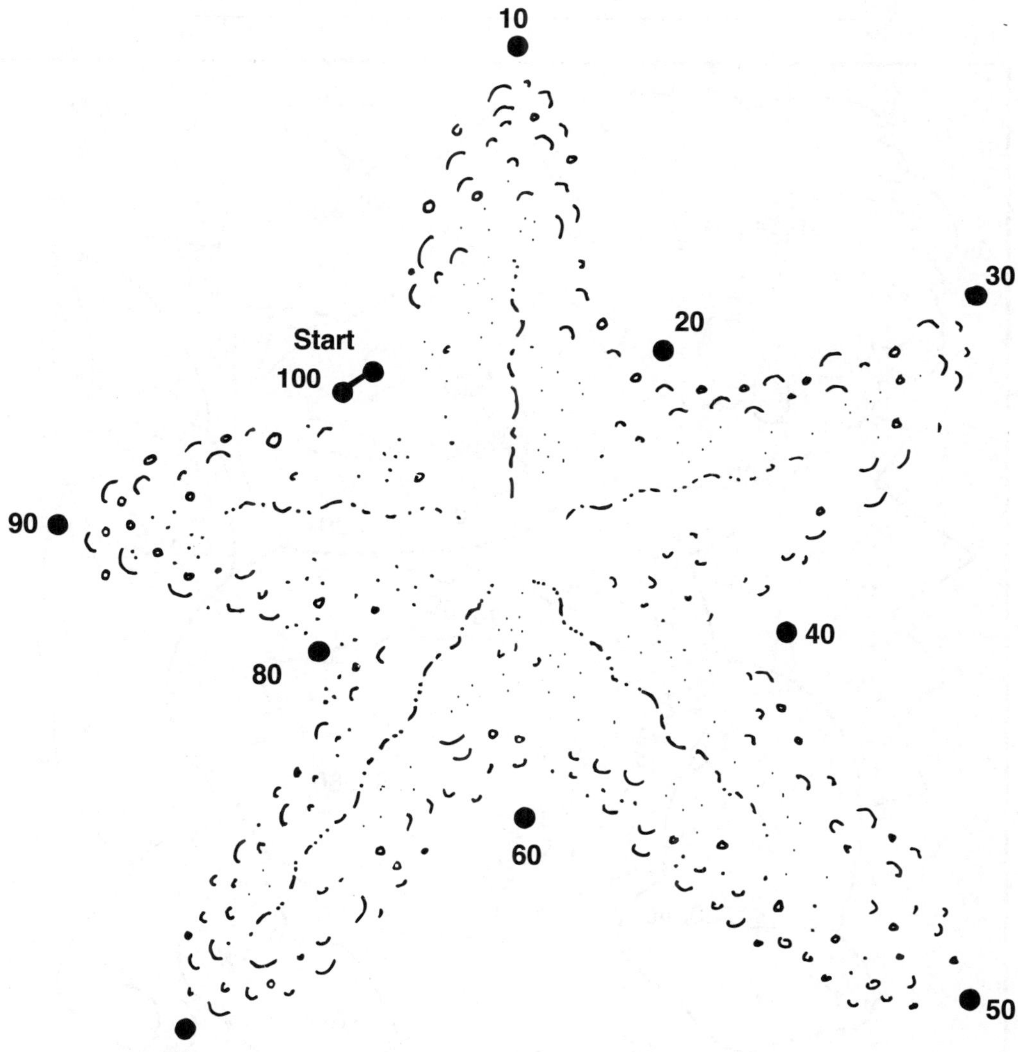

Give a Cheer!

Directions: Complete each number pattern. Color the puzzle.

10 = red   20 = brown   30 = green   40 = orange

Finding Groups of 10

Directions: Count how many ladybugs there are below. Write this number at the top. Then draw a line around each group of 10 ladybugs. How many groups have you made? Write this number in the square at the bottom.

How many ladybugs? ☐

☐ **groups of 10 ladybugs**

Ready · Set · Learn

What Comes Next?

Directions: Count by tens to find what comes next.

1. 10, 20, 30, ________

2. 50, 60, 70, ________

3. 20, 30, 40, ________

4. 70, 80, 90, ________

Directions: Count by tens to find the missing numbers.

5. 10, ________, 30, 40, ________, 60, ________

6. ________, 50, 60, ________, 80, ________, 100

7. 40, ________, 60, ________, 80, ________

8. Carole Ann has 10 snails. Rhonda has 20 worms. Their friend Robert has 10 lizards. How many creepy crawlies do they have in all?

☐ + ☐ + ☐ = ☐

Counting Backward

Directions: Count backward by tens to complete the pattern.

1. 52, ____ , 32, 22,

2. 70, 60, ____ , ____

3. 62, 52, ____ , 32

4. 91, ____ , 71, ____

5. 85, 75, ____ , 55

6. 43, ____ , 23, ____

7. 75, ____ , ____ , 45

8. 97, ____ , 77, ____

Directions: Find each difference.

9. 50 – 40 = ☐

10. 44 – 34 = ☐

11. 95 – 85 = ☐

12. 75 – 65 = ☐

Ready·Set·Learn

The Happy Tens

Directions: Counting by tens is quick and easy. Things that are quick and easy make people smile. Remember that 1 ten = 10 ones. Count the happy faces.

1.

 tens +  ones = ____

2.

 tens +  ones = ____

3.

 tens +  ones = ____

4.

 tens +  ones = ____

5.

 tens +  ones = ____

Patterns

Directions: Finish each pattern by filling in the correct numbers.

11	21	31	
24	34	44	
36	46	56	
27	37	47	
19	29	39	

Counting Up by 10s

Directions: Follow the path of numbers that count up by 10s.

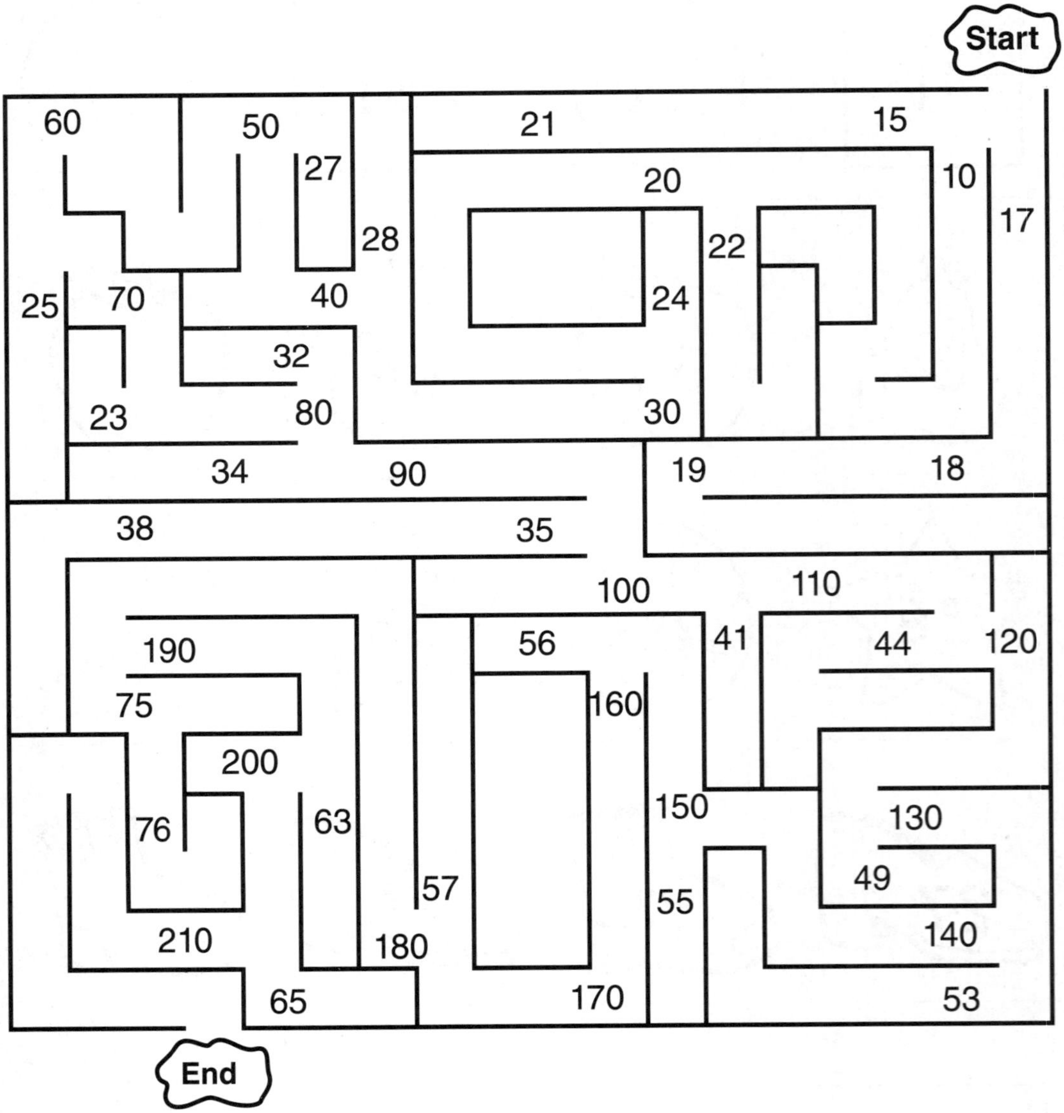

Joining the Dots by 10s

Directions: Here is a hidden picture. What do you think it might be? Start at 0. Count up by 10s and join the numbers in a line to make the picture.

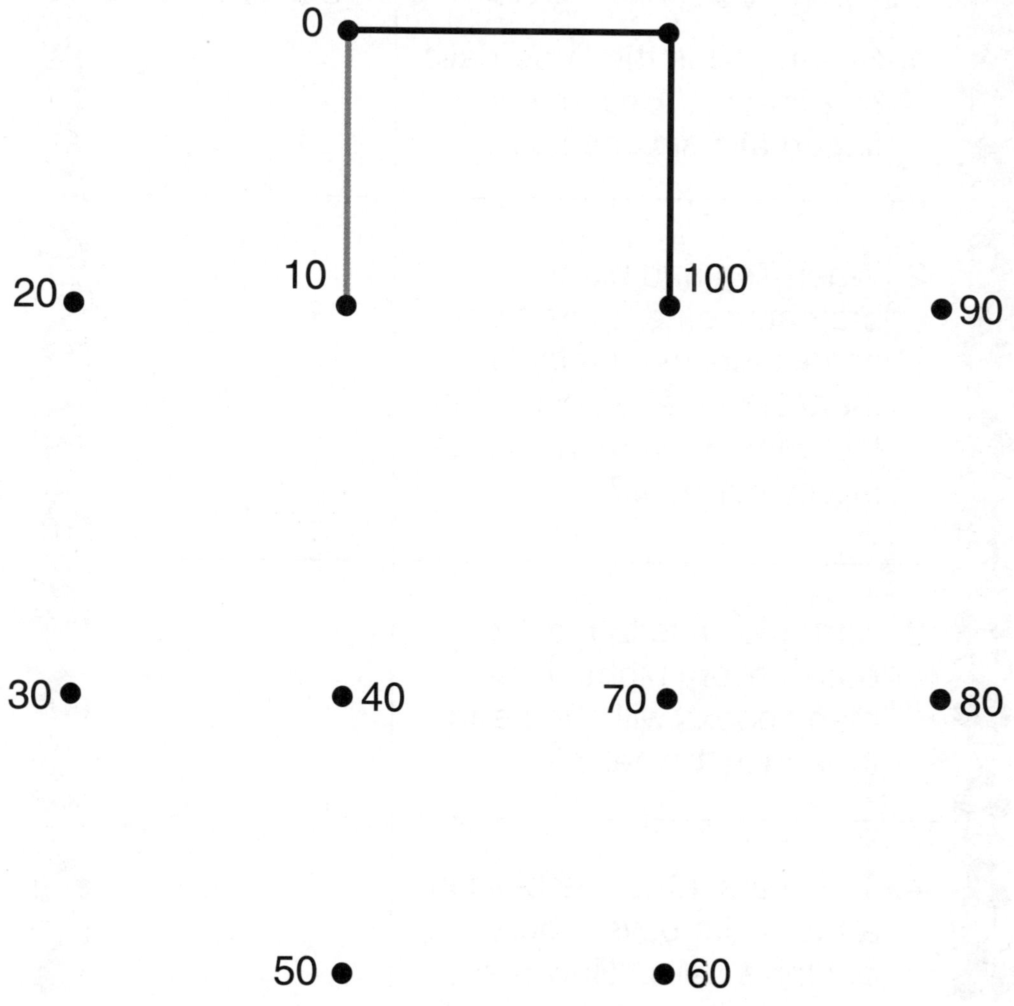

Skip Counting Problem Solving

Directions: Solve the problems. Draw or write in the space to show your work.

1. Susan paints the fingernails of 4 friends. How many fingernails did she paint?	
2. When Tim and his two brothers come home from school, his mom makes them take their shoes off at the door. How many shoes are by the door?	
3. Karly's goal is to read 2 books every night. How many books will she need to read in 1 week?	
4. There are 10 tennis balls in a box. Kim buys 7 boxes of tennis balls. How many tennis balls does Kim buy?	

Writing the Missing Numbers

Directions: Fill in the missing numbers on each snake, counting up by 2, 5, or 10.

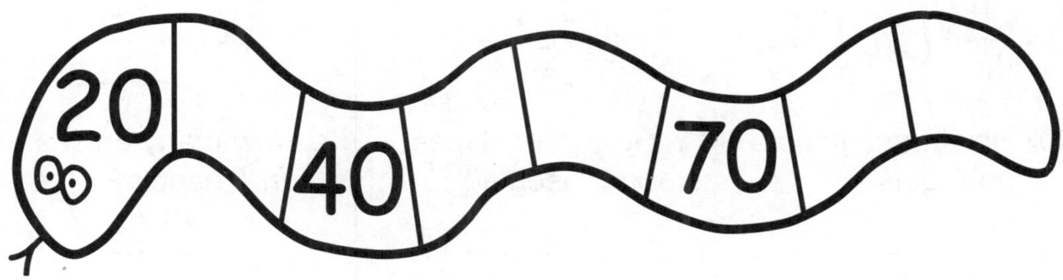

Ready·Set·Learn

Counting Body Parts

Directions: Skip-count in order to solve the problems. The first one has been done for you.

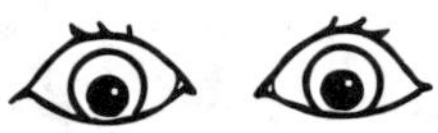 **1.** How many eyes on 7 boys? 14	 **2.** How many elbows on 4 men? ______	 **3.** How many mouths on 7 grandmas? ______
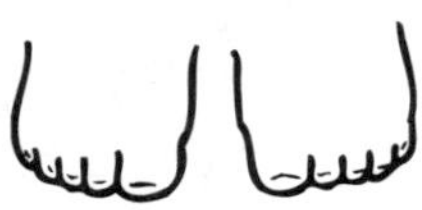 **4.** How many toes on 5 babies? ______	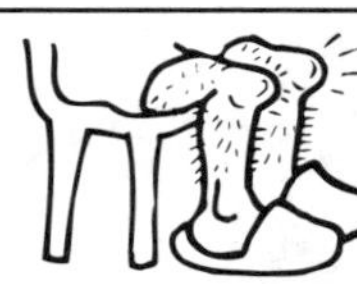 **5.** How many knees on 5 grandpas? ______	 **6.** How many feet on 3 brothers? ______
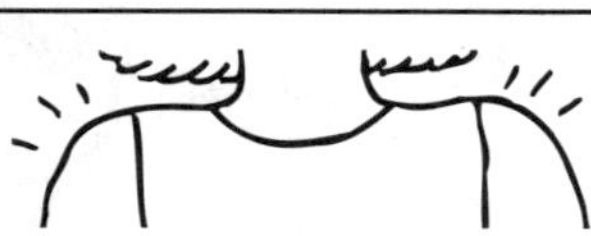 **7.** How many shoulders on 2 teachers? ______	 **8.** How many ears on 4 fathers? ______	 **9.** How many noses on 9 women? ______
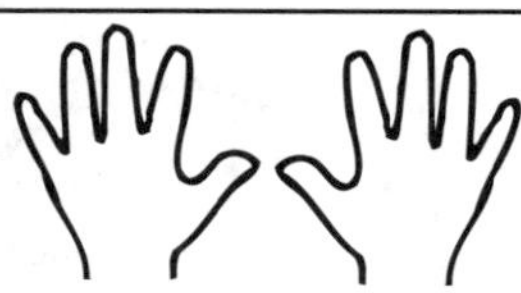 **10.** How many fingers on 6 girls? ______	 **11.** How many faces on 7 people? ______	 **12.** How many ankles on 4 people? ______

Jerseys

Directions: Finish the pattern to figure out what number is on each jersey.

Counting by 2s, 5s, or 10s

Directions: How many objects are in each group? Count the objects and write your totals in the boxes underneath as you go.

How many petals?

How many candles?

How many dots?

Skip It!

Directions: Can you help complete the patterns below? Fill in each blank with the missing number.

1. 5 ____ 15 ____ 25 ____ ____ 40 ____ 50

2. 10 20 30 40 ____ ____ 70 ____ ____ 100

3. 24 ____ 28 30 ____ ____ 36 ____ ____ ____ 44 46 ____ 50

4. 25 ____ 35 ____ ____ 50 ____ ____ ____ 70

On the Island

Directions: Complete each number pattern. Decide how you are counting. Color the puzzle.

Counting by 1 = blue **Counting by 2 = green**
Counting by 5 = yellow **Counting by 10 = brown**

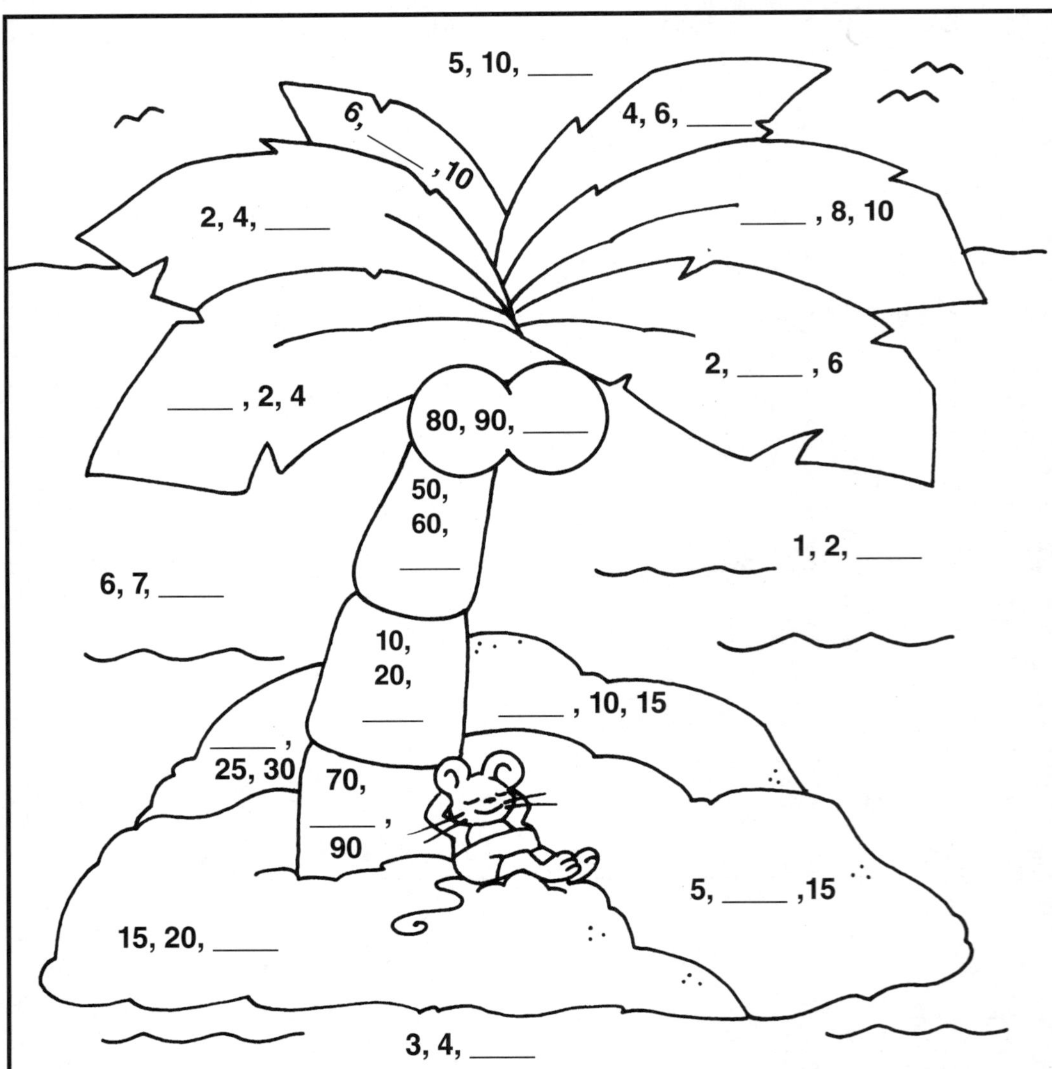

This Award Is Presented To

FOR

★ Doing Your Best

★ Trying Hard

★ Not Giving Up

★ Making a Great Effort